COMPARING
ANIMAL TRAITS

BALD EAGLES
PREY-SNATCHING BIRDS

LAURA HAMILTON WAXMAN

Lerner Publications ◆ Minneapolis

For Shaan, who deserves every ounce of this dedication

Lerner Publications Company
A division of Lerner Publishing Group, Inc.
241 First Avenue North
Minneapolis, MN 55401 USA

For reading levels and more information, look up this title at www.lernerbooks.com.

Photo Acknowledgments

The images in this book are used with the permission of: © David Schultz/Mint Images RF/Getty Images, p. 1; © Radius Images/Getty Images, p. 4; © Mark Miller/Photolibrary/Getty Images, p. 5 (top); © Natan Dotan/Moment Open/Getty Images, p. 5 (bottom); © Design Pics/Thinkstock, p. 6; © Zoonar/P.Jilek/Collection/Thinkstock, p. 7; © Gary Samples/Flickr RF/Getty Images, p. 8 (left); © David Tipling/Alamy, p. 8 (right); © S.J. Krasemann/Photolibrary/Getty Images, p. 9 (left); © Enrique R Aguirre Aves/Oxford Scientific RM/Getty Images, p. 9 (right); © Gerard Lacz/Visuals Unlimited/Getty Images, p. 10; © iStockphoto.com/MoniqueRodriguez, p. 11 (left); © Universal Images Group Editorial/Getty Images, p. 11 (right); © Laura Westlund/Independent Picture Service, p. 12; © Universal Education/Universal Images Group/Getty Images, p. 13; © Jared Hobbs/All Canada Photos/Getty Images, p. 14; © Emmanuel Rondeau/Alamy, p. 15 (top left); © Galen Rowell/CORBIS, p. 15 (top right); © Michael Sewell/Photolibrary RM/Getty Images, p. 15 (bottom); © Brian E. Kushner/Flickr Open/Getty Images, p. 16; © Robert McLean/Alamy, p. 17 (left); © Paul Reeves Photography/Thinkstock, p. 17 (right); © Brian E. Kushner/Moment RF/Getty Images, p. 18; Library of Congress (LC-USZC4-7214), p. 19; © Monte Comeau/Alamy, p. 20; © Don Johnston_BI/Alamy, p. 21 (top); © Gabriel Grams/Getty Images, p. 21 (bottom); © John Cancalosi/Alamy, p. 22; © Erich Schlegel/Corbis, p. 23 (left); © Berquist, Paul & Joyce/Animals Animals, p. 23 (right); © Darren Gidney/iStock/Thinkstock, p. 24; © Ron Niebrugge/Alamy, p. 25; © quentinjlang/iStock/Thinkstock, p. 26; © Chris Gomersall/Alamy, p. 27; © Les Piccolo/Flickr Open/Getty Images, p. 28; © iStockphoto.com/Charles Schug, p. 29 (left); © Matthias Breiter/National Geographic Creative/Corbis, p. 29 (right).

Front cover: © Jerryway/Dreamstime.com.
Back cover: © Tomtheodore/Dreamstime.com

Main body text set in Calvert MT Std 12/18. Typeface provided by Monotype Typography.

Library of Congress Cataloging-in-Publication Data

Waxman, Laura Hamilton, author.
    Bald eagles : prey-snatching birds / Laura Hamilton Waxman.
        pages cm. — (Comparing animal traits)
    Audience: Ages 7–10.
    Audience: K to grade 3.
    Includes bibliographical references and index.
    ISBN 978-1-4677-9507-4 (lb : alk. paper) — ISBN 978-1-4677-9629-3 (pb : alk. paper) —
ISBN 978-1-4677-9630-9 (eb pdf)
    1. Bald eagle—Juvenile literature. I. Title.
    QL696.F32W385 2016
    598.9'43—dc23   2015017440

Manufactured in the United States of America
2-43254-20620-11/16/2016

TABLE OF CONTENTS 4

Introduction
MEET THE BALD EAGLE 6

Chapter 1
**WHAT DO BALD EAGLES
LOOK LIKE?** 12

Chapter 2
**WHERE DO BALD
EAGLES LIVE?** 18

Chapter 3
BALD EAGLES IN ACTION 24

Chapter 4
THE LIFE CYCLE OF BALD EAGLES 30

Bald Eagle Trait Chart   31
Glossary   32
Selected Bibliography   32
Further Information   32
Index

MEET THE BALD EAGLE

A bald eagle perches on a tree branch overlooking a glassy lake. With its razor-sharp eyes, the eagle scans the water for fish to eat. Bald eagles are birds, a type of animal. Other types of animals you may know include insects, reptiles, amphibians, fish, and mammals.

Bald eagles often perch on trees.

A bald eagle soars through the air.

All birds share certain traits. Birds are vertebrates—animals with backbones. Birds are covered with feathers, unlike other kinds of animals. All birds have two wings and a beak. Birds lay hard-shelled eggs. Birds are also warm-blooded, so they keep a steady body temperature. The bald eagle shares these traits with other birds. But some traits set it apart.

DID YOU KNOW?
There are more than **SEVENTY** kinds of eagles in the world. Only two kinds live in the United States and Canada: the bald eagle and the golden eagle.

CHAPTER 1

WHAT DO BALD EAGLES LOOK LIKE?

Bald eagles are one of the largest raptors in the world. Raptors are also called birds of prey because they are excellent hunters. From beak to tail, bald eagles measure up to 3 feet (0.9 meters) long. They weigh around 9.5 pounds (4.3 kilograms). Their wingspan can be more than 7 feet (2.1 m). A bald eagle's powerful wings spread flat in flight. They allow it to soar, dip, and dive through the air.

DID YOU KNOW?
A bald eagle is named for its strikingly **WHITE HEAD.** Long ago, the word *bald* meant "white."

Bald eagles aren't actually bald. White feathers cover their head and neck. Dark brown feathers cover most of the rest of their powerful body. Their feet and beaks are bright yellow. So are their eyes. Eagles have excellent vision. Their eyesight is three to four times more powerful than that of humans. These birds can see the slightest movements of prey from miles away.

A bald eagle's wingspan is impressive.

BALD EAGLES VS. WHITE-TAILED EAGLES

A white-tailed eagle soars high in the sky. It slowly flaps its broad wings. White-tailed eagles and bald eagles are both deadly raptors. White-tailed eagles are about 3 feet (0.9 m) long, the same as bald eagles. They weigh up to 12 pounds (5.5 kg). The powerful wings of white-tailed eagles can be more than 8 feet (2.4 m) from tip to tip.

Like all raptors, bald eagles and white-tailed eagles have sharp talons for catching prey. Both eagle species have hooked beaks for tearing apart meat. White-tailed eagles and bald eagles have stiff white tail feathers. The feathers spread out like a fan. They help these birds steer and stay balanced in flight.

A bald eagle (*left*) and a white-tailed eagle (*right*) are about the same size.

COMPARE IT!

BALD EAGLES

VS.

WHITE-TAILED EAGLES

2.5 TO 3 FEET
(0.8 TO 0.9 M)

◄ BODY LENGTH ►

2.5 TO 3 FEET
(0.8 TO 0.9 M)

MORE THAN 7 FEET
(2.1 M)

◄ WINGSPAN ►

MORE THAN 8 FEET
(2.4 M)

YES

◄ SHARP TALONS? ►

YES

BALD EAGLES VS. GOULDIAN FINCHES

A Gouldian finch flutters to the ground from a low branch. With its small, red-tipped beak, it snatches seeds to eat. Gouldian finches live in Australia. They look different from bald eagles.

Gouldian finches are sometimes called rainbow finches.

Gouldian finches are much smaller than bald eagles. From beak to tail they measure just 5 inches (13 centimeters). They are also much more colorful than bald eagles. Gouldian finches often have a black, orange, or red head; a grassy-green back and wings; a yellow belly; and a purple chest.

Unlike bald eagles, Gouldian finches have a small, cone-shaped beak. Instead of tearing apart prey, this beak plucks and cracks seeds. The feet of Gouldian finches and bald eagles differ too. A Gouldian finch's foot has three slender toes pointing forward and one toe pointing back. The toes allow Gouldian finches to perch safely on branches. A bald eagle's four toes are curved and thick. They are strong enough to grip prey.

The bald eagle (*left*) and Gouldian finch (*right*) use their beaks for different purposes.

CHAPTER 2

WHERE DO BALD EAGLES LIVE?

Bald eagles live in North American forests near lakes, rivers, oceans, and other bodies of water. They usually choose forest homes where older trees grow close together. The older trees stretch high to the sky, giving eagles a good view of the land. Perched in the upper branches, they can spot prey miles away. The dense tree canopy also provides shade for bald eagles and protects them from bad weather.

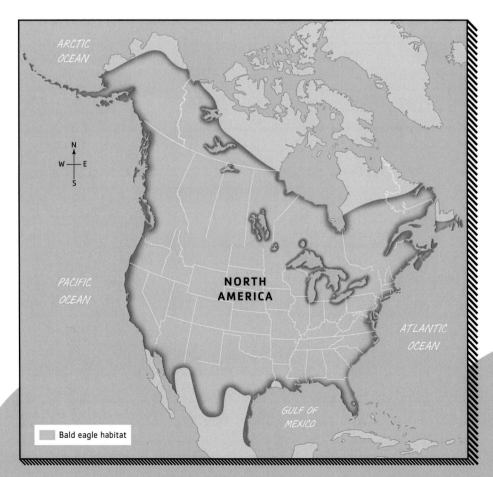

ARCTIC
OCEAN

N
W—E
S

PACIFIC
OCEAN

NORTH
AMERICA

ATLANTIC
OCEAN

GULF OF
MEXICO

Bald eagle habitat

Bald eagles usually live less than 2 miles (3.2 kilometers) from open water. That's because fish are an important food source for these birds. Bald eagles are carnivores. They hunt for a variety of small animals in their habitat.

A bald eagle snags a fish.

BALD EAGLES VS. SPOTTED OWLS

A spotted owl perches on a tree branch. Silent and still, it swivels its head at the slightest sound of prey. Like bald eagles, spotted owls are raptors that live in North America. They also live in a similar habitat.

Spotted owls often live in forests with old trees. Like bald eagles, spotted owls use the tallest trees as lookout spots for prey. They also rely on trees for cover from the weather.

A northern spotted owl perches on a tree in British Columbia, Canada.

A bald eagle (*left*) and a spotted owl (*right*) both catch prey in their sharp talons.

Spotted owls sometimes live near open water, like bald eagles. But the owls come to these bodies of water to drink, not to find food. Spotted owls are carnivores, the same as bald eagles. These owls mostly eat small forest mammals, such as the northern flying squirrel. They also eat some of the insects, small birds, and reptiles that share their habitat.

DID YOU KNOW?
Spotted owls aren't known for their great eyesight. They rely on powerful **HEARING** to listen for the slightest pitter-patter of prey.

BALD EAGLES VS. SAVANNAH SPARROWS

A Savannah sparrow gathers with its **flock** in an open, grassy field. Savannah sparrows are small, round songbirds. They live in a different kind of habitat than bald eagles.

Savannah sparrows live in grasslands covered with short and medium grasses. Unlike bald eagles, they avoid areas with too many trees. Instead, they seek open stretches of land. Savannah sparrows spend most of their days on the ground searching for food.

Savannah sparrows are **omnivores**. In the summer, they hunt for insects and spiders in the grass. In the winter, they eat mostly seeds.

A Savannah sparrow clings to a branch.

COMPARE IT!

BALD EAGLES

VS.

SAVANNAH SPARROWS

FORESTS ◀ HABITAT ▶ GRASSLANDS

YES ◀ LIVE NEAR OPEN WATER? ▶ NO

Fish, mammals, birds, reptiles, and insects ◀ MAIN FOODS ▶ Insects, spiders, and seeds

CHAPTER 3

BALD EAGLES IN ACTION

A bald eagle soars over a river with its wings extended. Then it quickly dives downward toward the water. As it approaches the river's surface, the eagle reaches down with its sharp talons. It snatches a salmon out of the water. As its talons pierce the salmon, the eagle uses its powerful wings to lift upward. It flies to a branch to eat its catch.

A bald eagle can carry heavy prey.

Although bald eagles are skilled fishers, they aren't choosy. They will take advantage of almost any opportunity for a meal. Ducks, rabbits, and lizards are just some of the animals they hunt and eat. They are also experts at stealing prey from other raptors. Bald eagles will scavenge for dead animals too.

When they aren't hunting, bald eagles roost in trees. They usually live alone but will sometimes roost together in large groups. As winter approaches, bald eagles in the North fly south to warmer weather. But bald eagles living in parts of the southern United States usually don't migrate.

DID YOU KNOW?
When the bald eagle became a symbol of the United States in 1789, not everyone was happy. Founding Father Benjamin Franklin disliked the way bald eagles stole prey from other birds. He thought the **TURKEY** should represent the nation.

An osprey catches a fish in its talons.

An osprey flies low over a lake, staring down with sharp, yellow eyes. Suddenly, it plunges feetfirst into the water. Ospreys are raptors that live all around the world. They behave in similar ways to bald eagles.

Like a bald eagle, an osprey's main food is fish. Both birds hunt for fish that swim near the surface of the water. Unlike bald eagles, ospreys may plunge completely underwater to catch a fish. As they fly away, they shake the water from their feathers.

An osprey tears into a large fish.

Ospreys eat small fish from head to tail, the same way bald eagles eat. This way of eating helps the fish go down more easily. It prevents a fish's spines and bones from getting caught in a bird's throat.

DID YOU KNOW?

Bald eagles often **STEAL** fish from ospreys. An eagle may bother an osprey until the smaller bird drops its fish. Then the eagle swoops down and snatches the prey.

BALD EAGLES VS. GILA WOODPECKERS

A Gila woodpecker hammers a cactus with its long, pointed beak. Gila woodpeckers are desert birds that live in the southwestern United States and Mexico. Gila woodpeckers and bald eagles do not behave in the same way.

Gila woodpeckers are omnivores. They eat mostly insects, but they also feed on cactus fruit, seeds, and other small animals. To find insects, Gila woodpeckers drill into wood and cactuses. They hammer deep holes with their strong neck and tough beak. They use their long, sticky tongue to pull out insects living inside. Some of these insects are harmful to cactuses. By eating them, Gila woodpeckers help keep the desert plants healthy.

Gila woodpeckers carve out larger holes in cactuses for shelter. They may also nest in holes in trees. The holes protect these birds from the intense desert heat.

Two Gila woodpeckers at a nest site

COMPARE IT!

BALD EAGLES

VS.

GILA WOODPECKERS

FISH AND OTHER SMALL ANIMALS

◄ MAIN FOOD ►

INSECTS, FRUIT, SEEDS, AND OTHER SMALL ANIMALS

SPIES ON PREY FROM ABOVE BEFORE SWOOPING DOWN

◄ HUNTING STRATEGY ►

DRILLS DEEP INTO TREES AND CACTUSES

Sharp talons

◄ HOW THEY CATCH PREY ►

Sticky tongue

CHAPTER 4

THE LIFE CYCLE OF BALD EAGLES

Bald eagles usually keep the same mate for life. But they do not stay with their mate all year long. They come together each spring for an amazing courtship flight. The male and female soar high in the sky before locking their talons together. Then they spin as they fall toward the ground. They separate just in time to avoid slamming to the earth.

DID YOU KNOW?

Over the years, a bald eagle nest can grow to be **9 FEET** (2.7 m) wide. It can weigh up to 2,000 pounds (907 kg). That's almost as much as a small car!

The mating pair builds a nest in a tree using sticks and soft materials such as grass and moss. They often reuse the same nest, adding to it each year. A female bald eagle usually lays one to three eggs each year. The eggs hatch after about thirty-five days. The chicks are covered with fluffy gray feathers, and their legs are pink. They grow quickly, gaining more than 6 ounces (180 grams) each day. In eighteen weeks, they are big and strong enough to care for themselves.

The appearance of young bald eagles slowly changes as they grow. The young birds have dark brown eyes and a dark brown head and body. Over time, their eyes lighten and become yellow. Their head feathers also get lighter each year. After five years, they look like their parents and are ready to mate. Bald eagles usually live for twenty to thirty years.

Bald eagle chicks don't look much like their parents.

BALD EAGLES VS. GREY HERONS

A grey heron wades through the water on long, graceful legs. Grey herons are large birds that live on many continents, especially Asia, Europe, and Africa. The life cycles of bald eagles and grey herons are similar.

Like a bald eagle, a male and a female grey heron work together to build a nest. The nest is usually in the branches of a tall tree. Grey herons often reuse the same nest, making it bigger each year.

A female grey heron lays about three to five eggs. She and her partner take turns incubating the eggs. Bald eagle mates also share this job. After the eggs hatch, the grey heron mates work together to care for their young, just like bald eagles. Young grey herons stay with their parents until they are nine to ten weeks old. They are fully grown after one year. The average life span of grey herons is five years.

A male grey heron finds sticks and grasses and brings them to the nest site. The female uses them to build the nest.

BALD EAGLES VS. RUFFED GROUSES

A ruffed grouse plucks berries from the low branch of a bush. Ruffed grouses are plump, brown birds that blend into their surroundings. Their life cycle differs from that of bald eagles.

Unlike bald eagles, a male ruffed grouse does his courtship performance alone. Standing above the ground on a log or stone, he flaps his wings to make a unique drumming sound that attracts a female. After mating, the male ruffed grouse leaves and does not help raise his chicks.

Ruffed grouse nests are shallow holes on the ground near trees and shrubs. A female ruffed grouse usually lays eight to fourteen eggs over a period of up to two weeks. They hatch in about twenty-four days. Ruffed grouse chicks can walk and find food right away. They are fully independent after sixteen to eighteen weeks. Ruffed grouses live for one to three years.

A ruffed grouse

COMPARE IT!

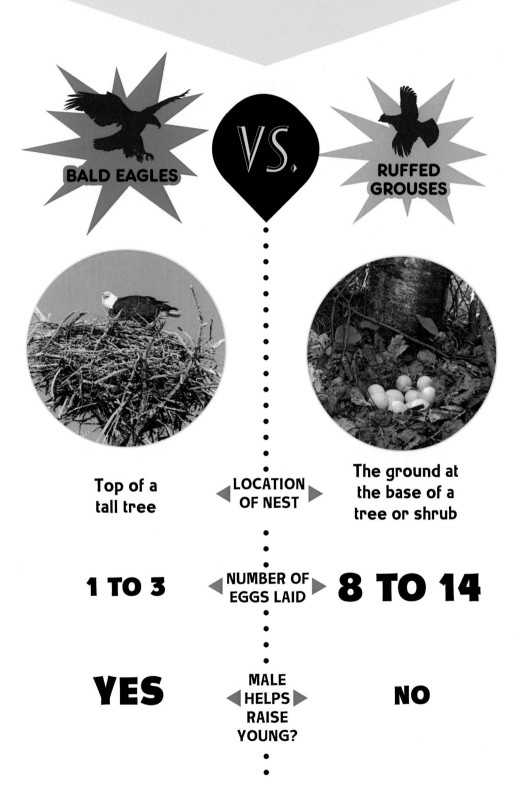

BALD EAGLES

VS.

RUFFED GROUSES

Top of a tall tree
◀ LOCATION OF NEST ▶
The ground at the base of a tree or shrub

1 TO 3
◀ NUMBER OF EGGS LAID ▶
8 TO 14

YES
◀ MALE HELPS ▶ RAISE YOUNG?
NO

BALD EAGLE TRAIT CHART

This book explores the ways bald eagles are similar to and different from other birds. What birds would you add to this list?

	WARM-BLOODED	FEATHERS ON BODY	LAYS HARD-SHELLED EGGS	RAPTOR	LIVES NEAR WATER	NESTS IN TREES
BALD EAGLE	X	X	X	X	X	X
WHITE-TAILED EAGLE	X	X	X	X	X	X
GOULDIAN FINCH	X	X	X			X
SPOTTED OWL	X	X	X	X	X	X
SAVANNAH SPARROW	X	X	X			
OSPREY	X	X	X	X	X	X
GILA WOODPECKER	X	X	X			X
GREY HERON	X	X	X		X	X
RUFFED GROUSE	X	X	X			

GLOSSARY

beak: the jaws and mouth of a bird. Beaks are sometimes called bills, especially when they are long and flat.

canopy: the upper layer of leaves and branches in a forest

carnivores: meat-eating animals

courtship: behavior used to attract a mate

flock: a group of birds in a particular place that belong to one species

habitat: an environment where an animal naturally lives

incubating: keeping eggs warm and under good conditions before they hatch

migrate: to move from one area or habitat to another. Animals migrate to find warmer or cooler habitats and to find more plentiful food.

omnivores: animals that eat both plants and meat

prey: an animal that is hunted and killed by another animal for food

raptors: birds that eat mostly meat and have excellent hunting skills, long talons, and powerful wings

roost: to settle down to rest or sleep

scavenge: to search for food, such as the remains of prey killed by other animals

species: animals that share common features and can produce offspring

spines: sharp, pointed parts on the outside of animals

talons: the long, sharp claws of raptors

traits: features that are inherited from parents, such as body size and feather color

wingspan: the length of a bird's wings from the tip of one wing to the tip of the other

LERNER

Expand learning beyond the printed book. Download free, complementary educational resources for this book from our website, www.lerneresource.com.

SOURCE

SELECTED BIBLIOGRAPHY

Alsop, Fred J., III. *Birds of North America.* New York: DK, 2001.

"Bald Eagle." Smithsonian National Zoological Park. Accessed July 16, 2015. http://nationalzoo.si.edu/animals/birds /facts/fact-baldeagle.cfm.

"Bald Eagle: *Haliaeetus leucocephalus.*" The Cornell Lab of Ornithology. Accessed July 16, 2015. http://www.allaboutbirds .org/guide/bald_eagle/lifehistory.

"Bald Eagle: *Haliaeetus leucocephalus.*" Seattle Audubon Society. Accessed July 16, 2015. http://www.birdweb.org /birdweb/bird/bald_eagle.

Martina, Leila Siciliano. "*Haliaeetus leucocephalus*: Bald Eagle." *Animal Diversity Web.* Accessed July 16, 2015. http://animaldiversity.org/accounts /Haliaeetus_leucocephalus.

FURTHER INFORMATION

Cuddy, Robbin. *All about Drawing Farm & Forest Animals.* Irvine, CA: Walter Foster, 2014. Learn to draw all kinds of different animals, including bald eagles.

George, Jean Craighead. *The Eagles Are Back.* New York: Dial, 2013. Follow a bald eagle's life journey in this colorfully illustrated book.

Johnson, Jinny. *Animal Planet™ Atlas of Animals.* Minneapolis: Millbrook Press, 2012. This book allows readers to travel around the world and explore the planet's incredible animal diversity.

National Geographic Kids: Bald Eagle http://kids.nationalgeographic.com/ animals/bald-eagle/#bald-eagle-closeup .jpg
Check out this *National Geographic* website for interesting bald eagle facts and photos.

Wildscreen Arkive: Bald Eagle http://www.arkive.org/bald-eagle/ haliaeetus-leucocephalus
Learn more about the lives of bald eagles with this website's photos, videos, and facts.

INDEX

bald eagle comparisons: vs. Gila woodpeckers, 22–23; vs. Gouldian finches, 10–11; vs. grey herons, 26–27; vs. ospreys, 20–21; vs. ruffed grouses, 28–29; vs. Savannah sparrows, 16–17; vs. spotted owls, 14–15; vs. white-tailed eagles, 8–9
bald eagles: diet, 13, 18–19; habitat, 12–13, 19; life cycle, 24–25, 26–27; size, 6; traits, 6–7
bird traits, 5

trait chart, 30
types of habitat: deserts, 22; forests, 12, 14, 17; lakes, 12; oceans, 12; rivers, 12